ABC
Animal Jamboree

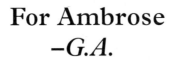

For Ambrose
–*G.A.*

To Stacey, Will, Dixie, and Dot
–*D.W.*

Originally published in Great Britain in 2009 by Orchard Books, London

ISBN 978-0-545-34269-8

12 11 10 9 8 7 6 5 4 3 2 1   11 12 13 14 15 16/0

Printed in the U.S.A.   08

First Scholastic printing, January 2011

ABC

Animal Jamboree

by Giles Andreae

Illustrated by David Wojtowycz

SCHOLASTIC INC.

New York Toronto London Auckland
Sydney Mexico City New Delhi Hong Kong

Aa Angelfish

Hello, I'm the angelfish, darling,
The prettiest thing in the sea.
What a shame there are no other creatures
As gorgeous and lovely as me!

Bb

Boa Constrictor

The boa constrictor's a slippery snake
Who squashes then swallows his prey.
He knows that it's not very friendly or kind,
But they do taste much nicer that way.

Cc Crocodile

When animals come to the river to drink,
I watch for a minute or two.
It's such a delight
To behold such a sight
That I can't resist chomping a few.

Dolphin

Dd

The wonderful thing about dolphins

Is hearing them trying to speak.

It's not "How do you do?"

As I'd say to you.

It's more of a "Click-whistle-squeak!"

Ee

Elephant

It's great to be an elephant,
All big and fat and round,
And wander through the jungle
Just elephing around.

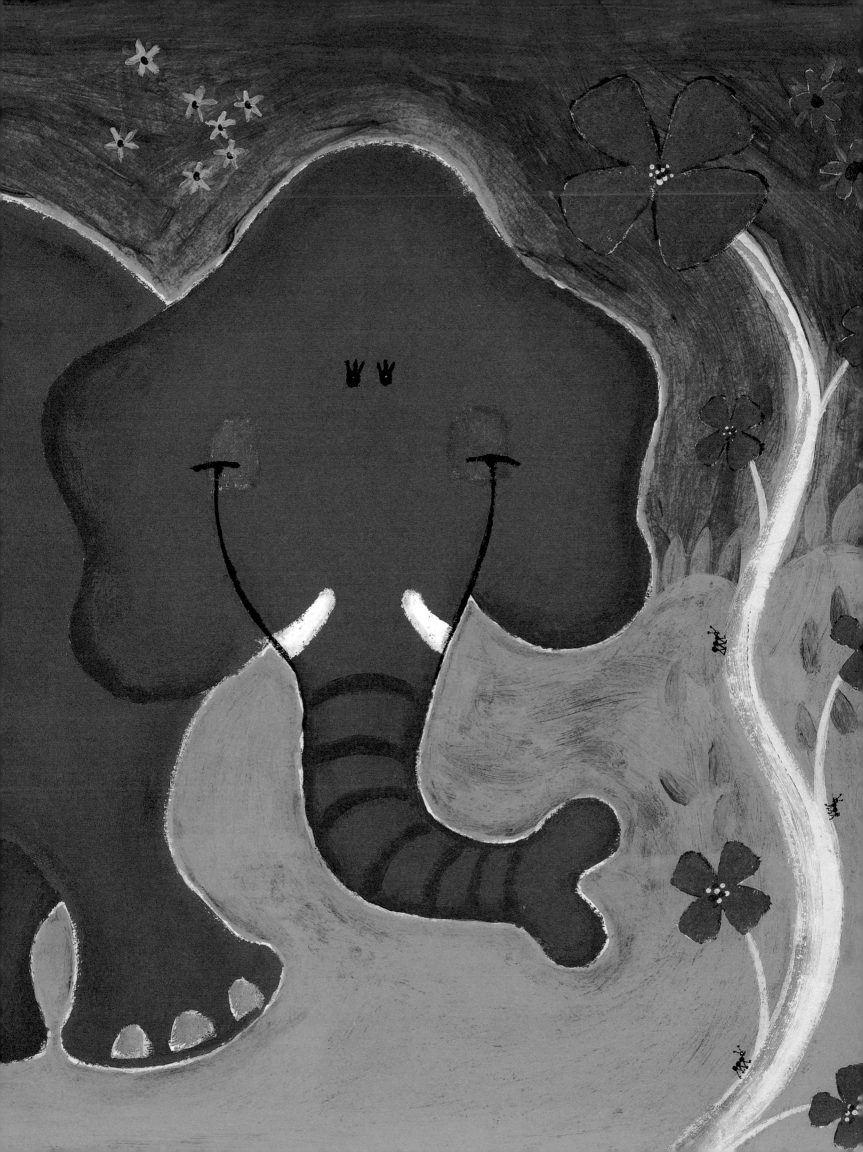

Ff

Frog

We may be green and slimy,
But I'm sure that you'll agree,
We're really great at hopping.
Can you hop as high as me?

Gg

Giraffe

Some animals laugh
At the gangly giraffe
But I hold my head up and feel proud.
I really don't care
When my head's in the air
And my cheek's getting kissed by a cloud.

Hh Hippopotamus

Hello, I'm a big happy hippo,
I sleep in the sun till I'm hot.
And when I'm not sleeping
I mooch in the mud,
Which hippos like doing a lot.

Ii

Iguana

We are both green iguanas,
Our bodies are covered with scales.
We've also got really cool spines down our backs
That run to the ends of our tails!

Jj

Jellyfish

The jellyfish just loves to jiggle,
Which other fish think is quite dumb.
She knows that it's not all that useful,
But jiggling's lots of good fun.

kangaroo

Kk

I'm the bouncy kangaroo.

Pleased to meet you! How d'you do?

And who's inside my pouch? That's right. . . .

It's Baby Joey holding tight!

r r r r

Lion

The lion's the king of the jungle,
Who quietly sits on his paws.
But everyone quivers
And shudders and shivers
As soon as he opens his jaws.

Mm Monkey

It's great to be a monkey,
Swinging through the trees,
And if we can't find nuts to eat
We munch each other's fleas!

Narwhal

Nn

The narwhal has a horn-like tusk
And so he seems to be
The ocean's swimming unicorn,
A marvel of the sea!

Oo Octopus

Having eight arms can be useful,
You may think it looks a bit funny,
But it helps me to hold all my children
And tickle each one on the tummy.

Penguin

We waddle around on our icebergs,

Which makes our feet slither and slide.

And when we get close to the water,

We leap with a splash off the side.

Qq

Quetzal

My tail feathers shimmer in glorious green
And look at my splendid red chest.
Of all the most beautiful birds that you've seen,
You must admit I am the best!

Rhinoceros

Rr

The ravenous rhino

Is big, strong, and tough,

But his skin is all baggy and flappy,

Which means that there's plenty

Of room for his lunch,

And that makes him terribly happy.

Ss Shark

I swim with a grin up to greet you,
See how my jaws open wide.
Why don't you come a bit closer?
Please, take a good look inside. . . .

Tiger

Tt

Beware of the terrible tiger,
You don't always know when he's near,
But his eyes shine like lights
In the blackest of nights,
And his growl makes you tremble with fear.

Uu

Umbrella Bird

My head has a crest of black feathers,
So when I look up at the sky
And see that it's raining
Instead of complaining
I just spread them out and keep dry!

Vulture

Vv

See me soaring gracefully
Across the clear blue sky,
Looking out for tasty treats
That catch my beady eye!

Ww

There's no other beast on the planet
As big as the giant blue whale.

He measures a massive one hundred feet long
From his head to the tip of his tail.

Xx

X-ray Fish

We like to swim around in shoals
And any food will do us.
Oh yes, we're called the X-ray fish
As you can see right through us!

Yak

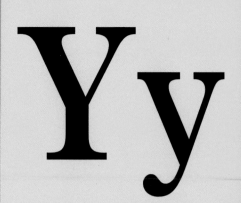

We live up in the mountains
Where the land is cold and bare,
So to keep us warm and cozy
We grow thick, long, shaggy hair!

Zz

Zebra

I could have been gray like a donkey
Or brown like my cousin the mule,
But instead I've got stripes,
Which my ladyfriend likes
Since they make me look handsome and cool.